30 Minutes
... To Motivate
Your Staff

D1454977

30 Minutes
... To Motivate
Your Staff

Patrick Forsyth

**KOGAN
PAGE**

YOURS TO HAVE AND TO HOLD

BUT NOT TO COPY

First published in the UK by Kogan Page, 1998
Reprinted 1999

Apart from any fair dealing for the purposes of research or private study, or criticism or review, as permitted under the Copyright, Designs and Patents Act 1988, this publication may only be reproduced, stored or transmitted, in any form or by any means, with the prior permission in writing of the publishers, or in the case of reprographic reproduction, in accordance with the terms and licences issued by the Copyright Licensing Agency. Enquiries concerning reproduction outside those terms should be sent to the publishers at the undermentioned address:

Kogan Page Limited
120 Pentonville Road
London N1 9JN

© Patrick Forsyth, 1998

The right of Patrick Forsyth to be identified as author of this work has been asserted by him in accordance with the Copyright, Designs and Patents Act 1988.

British Library Cataloguing in Publication Data
A CIP record for this book is available from the British Library.

ISBN 0 7494 2846 5

Typeset by The Florence Group, Stoodleigh, Devon

Printed and bound in Great Britain by Clays Ltd, St Ives plc

CONTENTS

The 30 Minutes Series

The *Kogan Page 30 Minutes Series* has been devised to give your confidence a boost when faced with tackling a new skill or challenge for the first time.

So the next time you're thrown in at the deep end and want to bring your skills up to scratch or pep up your career prospects, turn to the *30 Minutes Series* for help!

Titles available are:

30 Minutes Before Your Job Interview

30 Minutes Before a Meeting

30 Minutes Before a Presentation

30 Minutes to Boost Your Communication Skills

30 Minutes to Brainstorm Great Ideas

30 Minutes to Deal with Difficult People

30 Minutes to Succeed in Business Writing

30 Minutes to Master the Internet

30 Minutes to Make the Right Decision

30 Minutes to Make the Right Impression

30 Minutes to Plan a Project

30 Minutes to Prepare a Job Application

30 Minutes to Write a Business Plan

30 Minutes to Write a Marketing Plan

30 Minutes to Write a Report

30 Minutes to Write Sales Letters

Available from all good booksellers.
For further information on the series, please contact:

Kogan Page, 120 Pentonville Road, London N1 9JN
Tel: 0171 278 0433 Fax: 0171 837 6348

INTRODUCTION

If you think you can, you can.
And if you think you can't, you're right.
Mary Kay Ash

Management is about getting results *through* other people. As businesses and organizations face new and growing pressures and markets become ever more competitive, the job of the manager becomes more of a challenge.

Management can no longer rely (if it ever could) on just telling people what to do. Staff too have become more demanding. Yet the fact remains that managers cannot do everything themselves. The more complex or busy the business, the truer this is. Managers can only achieve their objectives by ensuring that everyone else is performing well.

In terms of both productivity and quality of work, the maximization of performance is vital. If people are not getting enough done, either through inefficiency or uncertainty, productivity will suffer and results may be delayed or jeopardized. If people are not delivering the required quality of work, then that too can directly affect the results of the section, or indeed of the whole organization. The details are important. It is not just the obvious effect of something major going really wrong, it is the trouble-shooting that may be necessary because one unthinking phrase is used in a document that, in turn, causes a communications breakdown which then leads to ... but you probably know the feeling.

Any failure may be aggravating, costly or worse simply within an organization. If it affects the outside world – upsetting customers perhaps – then the implications may well be worse.

So, managers must act, not just to ensure their people perform well, but to ensure they do so consistently and reliably. It is important too that people are largely self-sufficient, able to make decisions – good decisions – on their own and keep things running smoothly. If managers have to check every tiny detail and issue moment by moment instructions, then neither productivity nor quality achieved are likely to be good.

There is all the difference in the world between staff being able to do something and do it well, however, and being willing to do it and do it well. A major part of that difference is motivation. Managers need to motivate staff, and people working in a positive motivational climate are likely to work more effectively than those who are left to their own devices, certainly those who regard the way an organization or their manager works as restrictive, unpleasant or in any way demotivating. But motivation does not just happen. It is an active process. One that managers need to allow some time for on a continuing basis.

The aim of this short book is simple: to help managers achieve their objectives more certainly through the appropriate motivation of their people. It sets out to summarize the key elements of why motivation is necessary, what effect it can have and how to manage the process and create the specific motivation required. Along the way it uses examples, both for their own value (to use or adapt) and to show the range of what can be done. Some of what is reviewed is fundamental. Motivation is an integral part of management and must act as part of other ongoing management processes. But the emphasis is on the practical: those things that are simplest, have the most immediate effect and are least time-consuming to do. All managers are busy and looking at motivation this way is essential.

Motivation is a core skill of management. Done well, it allows managers – and their staff – to achieve more; and this is something that reflects well on the manager and which helps the organization meet its chosen objectives.

Patrick Forsyth
Touchstone Training & Consultancy
28 Saltcote Maltings
Heybridge
Essex CM9 4QP
Autumn 1998

1

A LITTLE THEORY

Many people, certainly in years gone by, took the view that getting performance from staff was a straightforward process. You told them what to do, and they did it. Period. And if that was, for some reason, insufficient, then it was backed by the power of management, effectively by coercion.

Management by fear still exists. In any economy with less than full employment the ultimate threat is being out of a job. But whether the threat is subtle or specific, whether it is just an exaggerated form of arm twisting or out and out bullying, even if it works (at least in the short term), it is resented. The manager's job is not simply to get things done, it is to get things done willingly.

The resentment factor is considerable. People fight against anything they consider an unreasonable demand. So much so that the fighting may tie up a fair amount of time and effort, with performance ending up as only the minimum people 'think they can get away with'.

Only if people *want* to do things and are encouraged to do things well, can they be relied on to actually do them really well. Motivation provides reasons for people to want to deliver good performance.

If this sounds no more than common sense, then that is because it is. For example, are you more likely to read on if I tell you that if you do not I will come round to your house and break all your windows, or if I persuade you that you will find doing so really useful and offer you some sort of tangible reward? (My intention is that you will find it useful, incidentally, but sadly there is no free holiday on offer.) Motivation works because it reflects something about human nature, and understanding the various theories about this is a useful prerequisite to deploying motivational techniques.

Theory X and Theory Y

The first of the motivational theories that is worthy of some note was documented by Douglas McGregor. He defined human behaviour relevant to organizational life as follows:

- **Theory X**: makes the assumption that people are lazy, uninterested in work or responsibility and thus must be pushed and cajoled to get anything done in a disciplined way, with reward assisting the process to some degree.

- **Theory Y**: takes the opposite view. It assumes people want to work. They enjoy achievement, gain satisfaction from responsibility and are naturally inclined to seek ways of making work a positive experience.

There is some truth in both pictures. What McGregor was doing was describing extreme positions. Of course, there are jobs that are inherently boring and mundane, and others that are obviously more interesting and it is no surprise that it is easier to motivate those doing the latter. Though having said that, it is really a matter of perspective. There is an old, and apocryphal, story of a despondent group of convicts breaking rocks being asked about their feelings concerning the backbreaking work. All expressed negative feelings, except one – who said simply, 'It makes it bearable if I keep the end result in mind – I'm helping to build a cathedral.'

Whether you favour Theory X or Theory Y, and Theory Y is surely more attractive, it is suggested that motivation creates a process that gets the best from any situation. Some motivation can help move people from a Theory X situation to a Theory Y one, thereafter it is easier to build on positive Theory Y principles to achieve still better motivational feeling and still better performance.

Maslow's hierarchy of needs

Another theory that helps describe the basic situation in which all motivational effort must be directed is that of Abraham Maslow. He wrote that people's needs were satisfied progressively. In other words, only when basic needs are met do their aspirations rise and other goals are set.

The first such needs were physical: enough to eat and drink, warmth, shelter and rest. In a working environment people need to earn sufficient to buy the answers to these. Next come needs of safety and protection: ranging from job security (one that is less easily met than once was the case) to good health (with the provision of health care schemes by employers now very common).

Beyond that, he described social needs: all those associated with working in groups and with people. The work environment is a social environment, indeed for some people it may represent the majority of the personal contact in their lives. Linked to these are a further level of needs such as recognition within the organization and amongst the people comprising the work environment, and the ability to feel self-confidence, self-fulfilment and to look positively to a better future, one in which we are closer to realizing our perceived potential and happier because of it.

However you define and describe this theory, it is the hierarchical nature of it that is important. What it says, again wholly sensibly, is that people's motivations can only be satisfied if this hierarchy is respected. For instance, it suggests that motivational input is doomed to be in-effective if it is directed at one level when a lower one is unsatisfied: it is thus of little use to tell people how satis-fying a job is if they are consumed with the thought that the low rate of pay makes them unable to afford basic essentials.

Again, this does not describe the whole process in a way that you can use to create the right motivation in your office, but it helps show one element of what is involved.

Hertzberg's hygiene/motivator factors

This last theory leads to a view of the process that links much more directly to an action-based approach to creating positive motivation. Hertzberg described two categories of factor: first, the hygiene factors – those that switch people off if they cause difficulty. And second, the motivators – factors that can make people feel good. Let us consider these in turn.

The dissatisfiers (or hygiene factors): these he listed, in order of their impact, as follows:

- company policy and administrative processes
- supervision
- working conditions

- salary
- relationship with peers
- personal life (and the impact of work on it)
- status
- security.

All are external factors that affect the individual (because of this they are sometimes referred to as environmental factors). When things are without a problem in these areas, all is well motivationally; if there are problems, they all contain considerable potential for diluting the motivational feeling.

It should be noted here, in case it perhaps surprises you, that salary is in this list. It is a potential dissatisfier. Would you fail to raise your hand in answer to the question: would you like to earn more money? Most people would certainly say 'yes'. At a particular moment an existing salary may be acceptable (or unacceptable), but it is unlikely to turn you on and be a noticeable part of your motivation. So too for those who work for you – more of this later.

It is, for instance, things in these areas that give rise to gripes and dissatisfaction that rumbles on: if the firm's parking scheme fails to work and you always find someone else in your place, perhaps someone more senior who it is difficult to dislodge, it rankles and the feeling is always with you.

There are, as we will see later, many things arising from these areas for managers to work at, and which getting right can be seen to make a positive contribution to boosting the motivational climate.

The restriction here is that these things are not those that can add powerfully to positive motivational feeling. Get things right here and demotivation is avoided. To add more you have to turn to Hertzberg's second list.

The satisfiers (or motivators): these define the key factors that create positive motivation. They are, in order of power:

- achievement
- recognition
- the work itself
- responsibility
- advancement
- growth.

It is all these factors, whether positive or negative and stemming from the intrinsic qualities of human nature, that offer the best chance of being used by management to play their part in ensuring that people want to perform and perform well.

Conclusions

It may seem from what has been said already that motivation is a complex business. To some extent this is so. Certainly it is a business affected by many, and disparate, factors. The list of factors affecting motivation, for good or ill, may be long, and that is where any complexity lies, but the process of linking them in terms of action is often straightforward.

The very nature of people, and how their motivation can be influenced, suggest five important principles for the manager dedicated to actively motivating people.

1. There is no magic formula

No one thing, least of all money, provides an easy option to creating positive motivation at a stroke, and anything that suggests itself as such a panacea should be viewed with suspicion.

2. Success is in the details

Good motivation comes from minimizing the factors that tend to create dissatisfaction, and maximizing the effect of those factors that can create positive motivation. *All of them* in both cases must be considered; it is a process of leaving no stone unturned, with all those found able to contribute to the overall picture being used.

At the end of the day, what is described as the motivational climate of an organization, department or office is the sum of all the pluses and minuses in terms of how individual factors weigh in the balance.

3. Continuity

The analogy of climate is a good one. As a small example of this, consider a greenhouse. Many factors contribute to the temperature inside. Heating, windows, window blinds, whether a door or window is open, if heating is switched on, and so on. But some such things – whatever they are – are in place and contributing to the prevailing temperature *all the time.*

So too with motivation. Managers must accept that creating and maintaining a good motivational climate takes some time and is a continuous task. Anything, perhaps everything, they do can have motivational side effects. For example, a change of policy may involve a new system and its use may have desirable effects (saving money, say), but if complying with the system is seen as bureaucratic and time-consuming, the motivational effect may be negative despite results being changed for the better.

Overall, the trick is to spend the minimum time in such a way as to secure the maximum positive effect.

17

4. Time scale

Another thing that must be recognized is the differing time scales involved here. On the one hand, signs of low motivation can be a good early warning of performance in peril. If you keep your ear to the ground you may be able to prevent negative shifts in performance or productivity by letting signs of demotivation alert you to the coming problem. The level of motivation falls first, performance follows.

Similarly, watch the signs after you have taken action aimed at actively affecting motivation positively. Performance may take a moment to start to change for the better, but you may well be able to identify that this is likely through the signs of motivation improving. Overreacting because things do not change instantly may do more harm than good. If motivation is improving, performance improvement is usually not far behind.

5. Bear others in mind

There is a major danger in taking a censorious view of any motivational factor – positive or negative. Most managers find that some at least of the things that worry their staff, or switch them on, are not things that would affect themselves. No matter. It is the other people who matter. If you regularly find things that you are inclined to dismiss as not of any significance, be careful. What matters to you is *not* the same as what matters to others.

If you discover something that can act for you, however weird or trivial it may seem, use it. Dismissing it out of hand just because it is not something that you feel is important will simply remove one factor that might help influence the motivational climate and make achieving what you want just a little more difficult. At worst, it will also result in your being seen as uncaring.

Similarly, what is important to you may not be to others. This is an important factor that any manager forgets at their peril.

Aiming for excellence

Finally in this chapter, remember that even the best performance can often be improved. Motivation is not simply about ensuring that what should happen happens. It is about striving for – and achieving – excellence. All sorts of things contribute, from the original calibre of the staff you recruit to the training you give them, but motivation may be the final spur that creates exceptional performance where there would otherwise only be satisfactory performance.

It is an effect worth seeking; and it is one multiplied by the number of staff involved. How much more can be achieved by ten, twenty or more people all trying just that bit harder, than can be by one manager, however well intentioned, doing a bit more themselves?

Motivation makes a real difference.

2

THE NEGATIVE SIDE OF THE BALANCE

This is the first area of detailed consideration for the manager. There is a list of factors (itemized in the last chapter), all of which must be considered. Each, in turn, gives rise to a variety – a plethora – of areas to consider. All of these must be dealt with on the one hand to minimize any negative effect and, on the other, to see what positive impact is possible here.

Company policy and administration

No one likes unnecessary administration or bureaucracy. And this is especially true when it affects them personally in a restrictive way or gives rise to unfairness. Usually as a manager you have two areas to worry about here, the circumstances of:

- **your own department**: here the task is to consider the motivational implications of every policy and administrative procedure you have in place or instigate. Every form that speeds efficiency may have downsides for those completing it. Every policy, however practical, may do harm as well as good.

  For example, a control system may be necessary, but the paperwork involved may be a real chore. If people do not understand the necessity and the advantages that may flow from it (perhaps because no one has explained), they will hate completing it – and may do so in a way that is incomplete or late. The impact will be worse if they feel no effort has been made to keep the system simple.

  Every element of every system should be thought through to ensure any demotivation is minimized. And systems must be monitored regularly to make sure they do not get out of date. Time passing and circumstances changing may make any system less effective, so review is necessary apart from the consideration of motivational impact.

- **the organization as a whole**: here the task is less to ensure that systems are right for your people, they may be instigated elsewhere, than one of communication.

  It may be necessary to explain – and endorse – central policies and systems (even those you do not like). It may also be necessary to make suggestions, in a way that acts in both the short and long term, to condition the effect on your people. Staff will always regard you as a weak, perhaps uncaring, manager if you apparently do nothing about matters that clearly inconvenience people or (which can happen) actually make it more difficult for them to do their jobs. Thus maintaining motivation

EXAMPLES

The examples that follow show both the extent of this area and give ideas of the action possible: forms, procedures, systems, standing instructions, rules (for example about: personal telephone calls, clocking in, dress codes or uniforms, protective clothing, cleaning of clothes, purchase of company product at a discount). This is an area where every individual manager in every separate organization can doubtless compile a long list. Those quoted merely aim to start that process.

includes fighting your corner for your section, even if this means difficult communications with more senior people. Again this is a matter of continuous review and action.

Supervision

If you are a manager, then supervision means you. How you work, and particularly how you interact with others, especially those who report directly to you, will influence the motivational climate. And it can do so for good or ill. No manager, however personable they believe they are, can assume that people will simply love working for them because it is just wonderful to do so.

This area needs conscious thought and action too. It is mentioned here to put it in its appropriate place on the overall balance; it is reviewed in more detail separately in Chapter 4.

Interpersonal relationships

There are groups of people within some organizations whose job is to get on with their own work and who have little interaction with others. More often, teamwork is important, and even if it is not, people will create social interactions because they like them.

A manager must work to try to create a team who, by and large, enjoy working together and make sure that none of the interactions between people cause problems or rankle in any way. Because of the nature of people this too is a full-time job. No group is wholly untroubled by friction, indeed some friction may well be constructive, but it needs to be kept in proportion.

How interpersonal relationships work starts with the way a team is put together – with recruitment and selection – and goes on throughout every aspect of their working together. It would be wrong to say that every group needs

---

Some factors can be used to create or stimulate communications between groups and within an organization. Notice boards and company newsletters or magazines are part of this; the process is also helped by canteens, Resource Centres, library and information offices, social clubs, health clubs or facilities, Christmas or anniversary celebrations, counselling services (for a range of things from overeating to outplacement).

An individual manager may be able to offer specific stimulus to the process, for example mixing technical and sales staff for product briefing meetings, or arranging a tour of certain departments for those who must liaise with them but do not normally visit them.

---

to be made up of similar individuals (again, variety can be constructive and creative), but obvious clashes should be avoided. Such could be one young member of one sex in a group which is otherwise older and of the other sex, or it might be one commuter always rushing for their train in the evening when the group thrives on a little social activity that overlaps the end of the day and spans office and pub. Examples such as these are selected to illustrate the range of factors potentially involved.

Working conditions

Productivity and efficiency are directly affected by how people work, and that in turn is affected by their work situation. Space, equipment and everything from air conditioning to whether chairs are comfortable all have an effect.

Here again, while no one expects every job to come with its own plush office, hot and cold running secretaries and unlimited expenses, people are demotivated if conditions are allowed uncaringly to make doing a good job more difficult. Expectations are affected by prevailing practice. For instance, you can readily think of equipment that has moved from being an exception to being 'essential', and is now resented if it is not there: for example mobile telephones, laptop computers etc.

Working conditions can be changed radically. For instance, some organizations claim dramatic increases in both productivity and motivation from what is called 'hot desking' (no individual work stations, and a much more organized and integrated open-plan environment); this shows just how broad an area this heading encompasses.

Everything that goes with the job should be included here, from whether you use machines or have a travelling 'tea lady' to how well various systems work. One item that is worth individual mention is the company car. Those who do not have one may regard those who do with envy. Surely any reasonable car is better than none? Not so. Company cars are a major source of dissatisfaction. Everyone who has one wants a better one, or wants it changed more often or to be allowed more choice in the make and model. Any seeming unfairnesses are quickly spotted – *why does he have that car, he only does a few thousand miles a year and here am I pounding up and down the motorway in a clapped out . . . ?* This is a matter of status as well as practicality; a good example of how certain factors have motivational implications in a number of different ways. So, the moral must be to set, and explain, policy very clearly in this area, watch it like a hawk and not expect motivational miracles because a car is a given. Cars in unexpected areas, however, may have a strong positive effect. I know managers who give their secretaries a small car, and gain considerable loyalty, retention and long-term cost saving as a result.

Be vigilant too about the tax implications of giving a company car, the rules can change and may negate any initial advantage.

Personal life

None of the best or most interesting jobs are, in my experience, nine to five. But if a job makes unreasonable or unfair inroads into people's private lives this will be resented. Prevailing practice is important here. If certain jobs typically make high demands, this may be regarded as normal, and this may mean people put up with it; but it does not mean they like it.

Organizations have to expect people to work hard in a competitive world, but there are limits. Eventually productivity tails down – there is a considerable difference between activity and achievement. Some people spend extra hours in the office, but not all of these are the most productive. The balance needs watching.

So too does the match between people and jobs. Is someone married, single, do they have a young family? All such factors, travel to take just one example, change the way in which the overlap between job and working life is regarded and need to be carefully watched.

Managers should remember that staff are people with lives outside their work (really!) and they like it if you acknowledge this by remembering and commenting on birthdays, asking how the children did in exams and buying a bottle of 'bubbly' when someone does something special – which might range from getting engaged to passing their driving test.

Security

Job security may or may not be motivational (some people *want* more risk if it produces greater rewards). But this is not the sense in which the word is used here. People like security in a variety of ways, and if it is not manifested in those ways they will be demotivated. This gives the manager another area to keep an eye on and to juggle with to achieve the net effect they want.

For example, a degree of security comes from:

- an organization with a clear mission and good communications
- clear job descriptions and terms of reference
- knowing what is expected of us and how it is measured
- working in an (effective) team
- working for the right kind of manager (see Chapter 4)

- decisive leadership
- no (unnecessary) secrecy.

Let me add a further comment about job descriptions. These are important, and not just because Personnel says everyone must have one. They set the scene for clear job purpose and communication; it is useful if everyone within a department sees everyone else's – including yours. They should collectively spell out how people must work together, where overlaps occur and should be viewed as working documents that may often be as useful in the everyday situation as much as they are part of the formal systems of the whole organization.

You can doubtless add to the list here. Again, the canvas here is considerable, and security is inherently fragile. For example, one decision agreed upon behind closed doors with no explanation can dilute security and escalate rumours very quickly. Yet there may be nothing sinister at work, and it might have taken only a moment to ensure the incident was not seen in this way and avoid the harmful effect.

Status

Like security, this can be a largely hidden aspect of people's motivation, but that does not mean it is unimportant; rather the reverse. People want to be thought of as important, doing something worthwhile. If necessary, people will create their own status (remember the convict building a cathedral). It happens too on production lines, where people – if they are not switched off completely – will often tell others just how vital their particular bit of the operation is.

So you need to worry about where people sit, how respect for age, seniority, achievement or long service is shown, what they are called, and so on. A manager must create respect for their people within an organization. This involves communication. A customer being told by a switchboard that a sales representative is not in (something the caller probably expected) because *they're only a salesman* is neither well briefed nor helping raise the status of a colleague in the eyes of a customer.

Problems may be deeply buried in this area: I once came across someone deeply demotivated because their spouse (who worked in a different field and company) had been promoted and now had 'Manager' on their business card, while they did not. It took a while for their manager to get to the bottom of it.

Salary

Yes, this is on the negative side of the balance. Are you that rare person who is totally happy with their current salary? More likely you would like it to be higher. *Existing* salary is rarely motivational. And if it is unfair (internally), out of line with similar jobs elsewhere or otherwise open to real criticism, then it can be a major demotivational factor. In one company I know, salaries are regarded as completely open: anyone can go into the Accountant's office and ask what anyone else earns – and be told. The main effect of this is to act as a control on how salaries are being set – there is no unfairness there, or gripes. I do not suggest this is right for every organization; but it bears thinking about.

Another example which says something about how salaries work is the following: freezing salaries for a year can give rise to two years of festering resentment (and thus needs a very good reason). As manager you may be paid to worry about the long term – the financial year – but if some of your staff, especially those who are younger, think

Friday week is a long way off, then such long spans of time will be regarded very differently by them.

So, motivation cannot be boosted, certainly in the long term, simply by throwing money at it. Of course, salary (in fact, total renumeration) is important. But it must be considered, just like every other factor, as part of a complex mix – contributing to the ultimate balance along with the other factors.

But you do not need to write off salary completely. A salary *increase*, especially one awarded for merit, is certainly motivational (and we return to that in the next chapter).

3

THE POSITIVE
SIDE OF THE
BALANCE

Motivation is not all about avoiding negatives, there are plenty of things that can be actively done to produce positive effects. As in the last chapter, we will use the list of factors identified in Chapter 1, commenting on them in order of influence.

Achievement

Everyone gets a kick from achieving something. I was pleased to finish writing the last chapter and press 'Save'. There may be very many such small, private satisfactions during your day's work; there will also be much greater factors (I will be even more pleased when the first printed copy of this book lands on my desk with a – small! –

30 Minutes . . . To Motivate Your Staff

cheque), these going right through to the satisfaction of a whole financial year well concluded.

Achievement is relative. Small things can assume a disproportionate importance. And that is fine, to an extent people create their own satisfaction. Though it is important that you provide people with sufficient benchmarks to have something to measure achievement against. Targets, formal and informal, are part of this; and they can be linked to almost anything: the amount a sales person sells, how well staff are trained or retained, cost saving, speed and efficiency, customer satisfaction, and more. The informal, simply saying – *let's make that even more tomorrow* – is important too.

Achievement is the most powerful motivator. But its power is enhanced many times when it is linked to the next factor.

Recognition

Recognition of achievement is a vital part of good motivation. It also sits best with good management. Unless things are well organized, people know what to do and have clear objectives, achievement and its recognition may be difficult.

Recognition of achievement can be minor and momentary – saying: *well done!* (and how many of us can put our hand on our heart and swear that we have done this as much as would have been useful over, say, the last month? Be honest.) Or it can be major and tangible – a salary increase (awarded for merit), a promotion or an incentive payment of some sort are all at the other end of the scale from a simple well done, and there are a great many forms of motivation that come between these two extremes.

The combination of recognition with achievement is an appropriate place to consider the whole question of

Taking recognition of achievement as one area, let us start with 'Well done' and other simple acknowledgements, and add that it is more powerful when said publicly (as during a departmental meeting) than in private; it can be endorsed by someone senior, in writing or in person, noted in the internal newsletter or pinned to the notice board.

Other extensions of 'well done' include employee of the month schemes (with a public identification as in hotels), certificates, badges and ties ... right through to a bunch of flowers or a meal or a drink.

This is as much for groups as for the individual. Part of keeping in touch (and what some now call 'management by walking about') involves motivation. It is as useful on occasion to speak to a whole department as to one member of it.

tangible rewards: that is everything, including salary, that is part of the remuneration package. This includes:

- **company cars**: which certainly have a value (though do not overlook the downsides – see Chapter 2 – or make unwarranted assumptions about their power)

- **commission**: this is usually defined as payment, most often on top of salary, linked to results (as with sales commission). This will only be motivational if it is personal (team commission is possible, but has less effect in raising individuals' motivation), if the payment is linked directly to activity and results and is easy to calculate and if the time scale is not too long (something paid monthly is better than something paid quarterly – and annual commission quickly becomes viewed as a right and has a very limited motivational effect). In addition, and this almost goes without saying, it must be significant as a proportion of income. These days it is as well to bear in mind family income, because what is judged as significant will, for many, relate to a household in which both partners are earning.

Remember too that there is a difference between what you might call commission (payment for past results) and an incentive (designed to boost future performance); only payments that meet the criteria described will work as an incentive and it is very easy for ill-judged schemes to become seen as a right or simply felt to be too insignificant or complex to be worth bothering about.

Commission or incentive 'payments' may be in other forms than money, gifts, theatre tickets . . . whatever. These need to be chosen to match what people want (but be careful about tax implications); some may lend themselves to group activity or the involvement of people's partners – as with travel (an overseas conference is a good example). Incentive schemes such as competitions can be fun and work well, though remember that if the same person always wins then others will quickly lose interest. Regular, overlapping, schemes – perhaps something different each quarter – work well and can be varied to keep up the level of interest they create.

- **assistance**: usually financial, this includes: rail season ticket loans, house or other loans at a special rate, and payment for things such as healthcare insurance, life insurance, travel insurance (covering personal/family travel as well as business trips), credit cards etc.

- **pensions**: a very important area these days (not least one affecting the original choice to take a particular job), with all the elements that make for a good pension potentially adding to its value

- **expenses**: that cover more than repaying monies spent on business (again watch the tax situation – for instance on things like petrol); a small example here is the scheme some companies have allowing people to charge books bought to read on overseas flights and trips (provided they go back into the company library afterwards). This is a little thing, but can be much appreciated

- **profit share, bonus or share schemes**: all these kinds of scheme can bind people to the organization and are used to link performance and payment

- **holidays**: these are important and link with family life (mentioned elsewhere). Both the length, and choice, of holidays and the way in which the organization operates around public holidays such as Christmas can be used motivationally (for example, in some organizations holidays increase – as may other perks – after a certain length of service).

The work itself

It helps if people like the work they do. This means that some jobs are easier to motivate people in than others; they are inherently more interesting. But if the work itself is dull, the workplace need not be; nor need what any particular work contributes to the results be insignificant.

In looking at your own staff, and in recruiting them too, you do need to think about round holes and square pegs. People who are in positions they are just unsuited for will always be difficult to motivate, and may never produce the productivity you want.

Bear in mind that other factors reviewed here influence this one. For instance, even dull work can be made more attractive if communication is good, if people know how they fit into the whole picture and that their contribution is important and valued.

Many managers take steps to extend the scope of the work, adding or involving additional aspects that are there, in part, to motivate. Schemes such as Quality Circles, or simply a suggestions box, may add to people's perception of their job and produce something useful at the same time. As an example, I remember being collected from an airport by a hotel car whose driver exemplified this idea. Essentially he was a taxi driver, but he clearly saw his job as that of a scene setter. His chatter on the way to the hotel informed, persuaded and made me look forward to the visit. It was done with great enthusiasm and made a considerable

---

A plethora of things come to mind that make the job easier, yet go beyond that:

- **equipment**: things like a fax, laptop computer, mobile phone or pager which can be used privately

- **convenience**: here we might include taxis home if you work late (also a safety measure), parking space, creches or child care provision

- **time-saving features**: a canteen (which may also promote social contact), on-site facilities (a shop, hairdresser, travel agent etc)

and other factors such as smoking or non-smoking policy (still a slightly thorny one, though the non-smokers seem to be winning), good lighting, plants, air conditioning, fans (in hot weather) and more can all be important. So too can the general atmosphere of the offices and things like there being somewhere nice to meet visitors.

---

impression. I bet it was more fun too to take this attitude than to just shut up and drive, producing a friendly response from guests (and larger tips?).

Responsibility

This ties in with the earlier example. My hotel driver was taking on more responsibility than just that of driver; and everyone gained. Most people enjoy responsibility – having something that is 'theirs', they 'take ownership', to use current jargon, and put more into something as a result.

In one organization they found that simply requiring people in a clerical office to sign their own letters with their own name, instead of preparing everything for signature by a manager, brought an immediate increase in productivity and accuracy.

There are links here to organization, work allocation and delegation. Giving people responsibility prompts their giving greater thought to their work and thus, very often, produces greater creativity. Managers who have a team of people should use them. You are not paid to sit and have all the ideas necessary to keep your department or what-ever running efficiently, and then just tell people what to do. But you probably *are* paid to make sure there are suffi-cient ideas to make things work.

Give people responsibility – ask – and you might be surprised how creative they can be. Perhaps there can only be one departmental manager, but there can surely be a host of subsidiary responsibilities, people in charge of projects, becoming your 'expert on . . . ' (an industry, customer type, IT development etc), briefing newcomers, maintaining records or updating information, and so on. And in every case this can potentially improve motivation and performance.

> The key thing here is perhaps projects: getting individuals involved, giving them things to do – to think about, check out, investigate, study, suggest, and so on – that are theirs, and referring to them as such.
>
> You will likely need a constant supply of such projects, overlapping, involving different people and linking, of course, to other areas such as training or innovation.

Advancement

People like to feel they are making career progress. Taking on additional small responsibilities may be part of that. So too is the way you organize and use the organizational hierarchy. Promotion is, of course, motivational. Grades and titles may be used to create sufficient levels so that people are able to rise and rise again. This may assist retention of good staff, it is in its way a form of recognizing achievement and it works well. In Sales for example, maybe there are Sales Executives, Senior Sales Executives, Account Managers and Key Account Managers. Or more. In part, such an arrangement may reflect the different jobs to be done, in part, it may be to provide a number of steps up. Such divisions need to be real, and linked to salary and terms and conditions as well as titles.

Work at giving people something to aim at, regular changes and evidence of real progress and they will stay longer and work more effectively than if they think they are in a rut. It is said there is all the difference in the world between five years' experience and one year's experience multiplied by five; and everyone wants the first of these.

Growth

Motivational theory differentiates between advancement and growth, one being progress within a current employer's organization, the other movement out to a better job. It might rightly be claimed that for large organizations there is an in-between area, characterized by someone moving from the consumer to the industrial division, or from London to the Asia Pacific HQ in Singapore.

Good motivators make people leave. Think about it. If no one ever left your team, what would it mean? Probably that people were all too mediocre to get better jobs. Of course, for the most part, people move on eventually. The trick is to build a first-class team (one whose members can ultimately get better jobs elsewhere if there are no internal promotion opportunities), but to retain them and maximize their performance as long and as much as possible.

Sometimes, perhaps with high calibre sales or technical staff, the industry norm is for fast turnover; in such a case just getting people to stay an average of, say, three years rather than two may be worth a considerable amount of money.

The full mix

As with the negative factors, what is important here is the net effect of all the influences, ultimately of the positive and negative together. The way motivation works is thus progressive and cumulative – every small factor may add a weight to the balance that ends up making the overall motivational climate what we want – and what our people want.

There are already many factors to consider here, the next two chapters add others that can also affect the total picture.

4

THE CONTRIBUTION OF MANAGEMENT STYLE

The kind of manager you are will certainly affect the ease with which you can motivate people and thus the time and effort involved in achieving results. Perhaps the first principle any manager should adopt is to be, and remain, well informed about the prevailing motivational status of any group for whom they are responsible.

There is more to this than simply asking. Indeed, just saying 'Anything worrying you?' to people, especially when there is, is not always likely to get a straight answer. People may want to tell you that you are getting right up their nose in some way, but bite their tongue, or they may not mention things they feel you would see as trivial. You need to be more subtle in investigation. Read between the lines, observe people's behaviour and how they react to things. Use the grapevine, gleaning informal comment to put alongside – and weigh carefully with – harder evidence.

Constant vigilance is useful, both to avoid missing opportunities to add positively to the situation, or to avoid unrest creeping up on you and only presenting itself when it has become a significant problem.

Employee opinion polling

Some organizations use a form of research to occasionally take the motivational temperature, as it were. If employees are given an opportunity to make their feelings clear, whether verbally or in writing (it may involve questionnaires), they will often take it – *providing* it is anonymous. This means that for best effect such surveys must be conducted separately from the management hierarchy, with an independent research company or consultant interfacing with the people concerned.

Such research may be particularly useful in times of change. What do people *really* think about the organization being sold, merging or moving to the other side of the country for instance? Money spent on such research may well represent a wise use of funds; certainly if the alternative is ignorance of something crucial which festers and causes major problems later.

The very fact that the organization does such a thing may be viewed as motivational. Though remember that a view will be taken of the project overall and people will look particularly for the action, if any, that follows the findings. Testing the water, then doing nothing, is unlikely to inspire any kind of good feeling.

The manager we want

Managers must manage. It is a process that demands some personal clout. But there is, in fact, an overlap between the characteristics staff approve and look for in the 'ideal' manager, and effective management. A good manager is fair, approachable, decisive, respects their staff and their point of view, is honest (and not unnecessarily secretive). Good communication is also very important. So too is people feeling they benefit positively from the relationship.

High on the list, people value consistency. If you run hot and cold, are sweetness and light one minute and doom, gloom and overbearing the next, people will understandably find you difficult to relate to. It helps too if any manager is seen as being good at their job. And, despite the old saying that you do not have to be able to lay eggs to be a chicken farmer, it helps if you at least understand the details of the tasks others have to work on.

Note too that the most motivational style aims high. People like to work in an environment of success in which challenges are set, people pull together and see the results of their efforts. They do not like 'passengers' being tolerated, and this has implications for managing people.

If some of these characteristics are not your natural character, then you may need actively to inject a bit more of them into your style. Think of what you would want from your manager; it works both ways. The remainder of this chapter looks at particular elements of management style that are disproportionately important in their motivational effect.

Communications

Being on the receiving end of good, clear communications is certainly motivational. Organizations characterized by people never really knowing what is going on, not being clear about objectives, policy or instructions rarely show evidence of high morale.

Because communication is inherently difficult (when was the last occasion on which you spent unnecessary time sorting out the results of some communication breakdown?), it needs thought and care. The following details are, like all such factors, important to the way the communication is received and judged:

- choice of communications method (eg memo or meeting)
- clarity of message (eg sufficient background)
- building in opportunity for feedback (or not)
- timing (eg ahead of the rumours?)
- who is communicated with (and who is not?).

Seeking comment, but conditioning the request – *I think this is a good idea, what do you think?* (with the sub-text seeming to be: disagree if you dare) – is certainly not motivational. Meetings make a good example and involve a whole panoply of communications situations. Do you like sitting in a meeting that starts late, that is rushed, disorganized and run without firm chairmanship so that no one feels able to put their point, or is not listened to if they do? No. And nor do the people who attend your meetings.

If you are a good communicator, if you write well and present your ideas well, know the rules of chairing a meeting and bring care and concern for the motivational implications of your every communication, you will find the advantages to your staff are appreciated.

Finally, informal communication is as important as formal. A good manager does not just keep people informed through discussion and sending memos (indeed, too many of those can be demotivational), they make the workplace fun. This is not overstating the point. Business is a serious business, but this should not make it dull. Most people spend more time at work than in any other way, they want it to be fun and managers who recognize this will motivate better than those who do not.

Consultation

This leads on from communication. People like to be consulted. They believe their opinions matter and that their ideas might be useful. And they are right. So adopting a consultative approach to management boosts motivation, and helps with what you are trying to achieve as well.

Of course, there are some things about which there is no merit in engaging in elaborate consultation, so in order to give time to the others where it is worthwhile you must select which goes in which camp. *Not* consulting on some things can be motivational, if people understand that this is done to give consultation time to other, more important, topics. Having done that, consulting can be very useful. Two heads really are often better than one; well conceived and executed, consultation within a team works.

You may usefully build consultation into regular procedures – the departmental meetings you already hold perhaps – or convene formal sessions just for this process. A useful part of it is essentially informal: stopping someone on the stairs just to ask 'What do you think about ... ?' All types of consultation have their place and will be appreciated.

There is one danger here: the kind of manager who consults and then passes on others' ideas around the organization as their own is deeply resented. Do not try to get all the credit. Being generous with the credit, for example labelling something as a subordinate's idea even when you made a major contribution or cajoled them into the thinking that produced it, is powerful motivation. After all, you get the credit for creating and maintaining a first-class team. If you want to make things happen, use the giving of credit to boost idea generation and motivation in parallel. It provides a powerful combination.

Development

Top of the list of almost any survey I have ever seen asking people: 'What makes a good manager?' is a comment about wanting to work for 'someone I learn from'. No one wants to stand still, and we all know the thought, mentioned earlier, that there is an important difference between five years' experience and one year's experience repeated five times. Which would you choose?

Development – training in all its forms – is motivational. Again, this is something with dual purpose. Developing people's skills is useful to the organization as well as to individuals; it can positively boost results and motivation together.

From the management point of view, it perhaps makes good sense to divide the methodology into two: individual mentoring and group development:

● **mentoring**: a mentor is someone who spends time, individually and often informally, with people to help them increase their experience and improve their competencies. Mentoring takes some time, but the results and following good motivation can be very worthwhile.

You need to relate this activity to some sort of overall development plan, and ensure that the whole process grows in effectiveness through the momentum and continuity of the process. Your staff will get used to these informal sessions and, finding them useful, will work at getting more from them. Just a ten minute digression during a meeting convened to progress some project may be necessary. Alternatively, you may be able to think of ways to incorporate advice and assistance into normal ongoing business processes. For example, to include an element of development activity on an important topic, some managers create a formality about certain internal meetings, making staff deliver their points as formal 'on your feet' presentations. This is an important skill, one helped by practice – doing this and adding a few words of critique or encouragement adds only a few moments to the meeting and is useful for all concerned.

- **planned development activity**: here the range of options is vast. People can attend courses (arranged 'in-house' or as 'public' events), but a host of lesser things are useful also. You can recommend staff read a business book, go to a showing of a training film (some companies have in-house showings at lunchtime), attend a conference, trade fair or other event, or work through some programmed training material (say, on CD-ROM).

All such activity can be made motivational, provided it is relevant and useful. Introducing new skills, some with an eye on the future rather than immediate needs, updating or upgrading others, correcting weaknesses

47

and building on strengths – all can be part of your overall motivation.

Remember, training and development do not have to appear as such, it is often more useful for someone to be involved in a project from which they will learn something – so the motivational effect of development can pervade many management processes. Here mentoring and development overlap.

Delegation

Who do you want to work for? Someone who is a good delegator or someone who is not? No contest; and those who work for you feel the same. If you are busy, and most managers are, then delegation can help you fit more in as well as allowing you to concentrate on key issues. It also ensures that things are regularly exposed to new thinking and new approaches; this is in major part how organizations change, grow and improve. Do you really believe you have a monopoly on common sense? And that no one can do things as well as you can? More often fear of someone doing something better than us is a prime reason why delegation does not happen as much as it should (be honest!).

Of course, delegation needs to be carried out effectively:

- selecting the appropriate task
- selecting the right people
- giving clear, well-communicated, briefings
- building in agreed, planned checks, if necessary
- not watching every move
- evaluating the results afterwards.

When it works well, it helps you by freeing up time that can be spent on key tasks. It helps staff by giving them new challenges, new tasks to handle as part of their work portfolio, and helping to develop or improve new skills and evolve new approaches in the process.

Appraisal

Let us be honest. Not every appraisal meeting held in every organization is constructive and useful. Too often they are regarded as academic and a waste of time (and often as worrying) by both those who run appraisal meetings and those who attend them. Yet, when well conducted, they represent a major opportunity.

How can a job be satisfying if the incumbent has no idea whether what they are doing is well regarded or not? The principle of achievement and recognition of achievement has already been touched on. It is a powerful motivator.

Appraisals, both the once or twice a year formal sessions that are typical in many organizations and the ongoing informal discussions that may sensibly be included as part of the process, can be so useful. They act to:

- review the past year
- plan the next
- formalize training and development plans
- spark ideas
- relate to long-term career development.

They are often, though not necessarily rightly, linked to review of salary and other rewards (note: there is a strong case for separating the two things to allow the appraisal meeting to concentrate on its practical review of practice and change for the future).

The better the appraisal system, and the more constructively you run appraisal meetings for which you are responsible, the more you will get from the process in terms of positive motivation.

This is not the place to go into detail, but the key rules are:

- ensuring the system used is logical, sound and focused on change for the future

- planning how you will conduct meetings in advance

- giving due notice and briefing to those being appraised to allow them to prepare

- ensuring the majority of the time is allowed for the person being appraised to talk (it is not simply an opportunity for you to tell them things), and is focused on the future not the past.

Reviewing the past is only useful as a way to make future operations more certain – viewed this way appraisals can be constructive, useful . . . and motivational.

The motivational manager

The factors reviewed here sit alongside the detailed action stemming from the positive and negative sides of motivation (reviewed in Chapters 2 and 3). The manager who is a successful motivator both sees the broad picture and gets the details right. They also see motivation as an ongoing process and recognize the cumulative effect of all that is involved.

Habit is a powerful ally to good practice here. Whether it is thinking of the motivational implications before circulating details of some reorganization or policy change, or simply remembering to say 'Well done', or its countless equivalents, sufficiently often – all these things can begin to be an automatic element of the process of management.

But remember, habit may assist the process, but only due consideration – and some creativity – can maximize its effectiveness.

Finally, in the last chapter, we will look at processes that help make positive motivation more self-generating, and thus more likely to be sustained.

5

INVOLVEMENT AND EMPOWERMENT

The word empowerment enjoyed a brief vogue in the late 1990s, as one of a succession of management fads that, if you believe the hype, solve all problems and guarantee to put any organization on the road to success. If only. On the other hand, there is sense in the idea of empowerment. It may not solve everything, but it is useful and it does provide additional bite to the prevailing motivational feeling.

Empowerment in action

Rather than give leaden definitions, let us start with an example. The Ritz-Carlton have enjoyed good publicity not only for the undoubted quality of their many hotels, but for a particular policy they operate. Say you are staying in one of their hotels and have (perish the thought) something to complain about. So, reeling from the stench from your minibar or whatever, you stick your head out of your room into the corridor and take up the matter with a passing chambermaid.

Now whoever you were to speak to, the procedure would be the same. *Every* single member of the hotel's staff is briefed to handle your complaint. They do not have to find a supervisor, check with the manager or thumb through the rule book. They sort it. As they think fit. And they have a budget to do so – every single member of staff can spend so many dollars (I think it started as $500, but has no doubt changed) instantly, and without any checks, to satisfy a guest's complaint.

So, to continue our example, if the minibar was dirty they could summon someone to clean it at once (even if that meant paying overtime), refill it with complimentary drinks and throw in a free bottle of fine wine and a bowl of fruit on a side table to make up for the inconvenience. Such staff are empowered.

It is an approach that gets things done. It regards staff as a key resource, not only one to get tasks completed but one who can, in many ways, decide just how they get it done. The empowerment approach goes way beyond simple delegation and plays on the appeal of responsibility to the individual to get things done and done right. It works in part because staff like it – being empowered is motivational.

Behind empowerment

On the other hand, empowerment does not allow managers to abrogate their responsibility, nor does it represent anarchy, a free-for-all where anything goes. The chambermaid (mentioned above) does not have the right to do just anything, only to select, or invent, something that will meet the customer's needs and which does not cost more than the budget to implement.

Staying with our hotel example, consider what must lie in the background. Staff must:

- **understand guests**, their expectations and their likely reaction to difficulties (and how that might be compounded by circumstances – having to check out quickly to catch a flight, for example)

- **be proficient at handling complaints** so as to deal with anything that might occur promptly, politely and efficiently

- **have in mind typical solutions** and be able to improvise to produce better or more appropriate solutions to match the customer situation

- **know the system**: what cost limit exists, what documentation needs completing afterwards, who needs to be communicated with etc.

The systems – rules – aspect is, however, minimal. There is no need for forms to be completed in advance, no hierarchy of supervisors to be checked, most of what must happen is left to the discretion of the individual members of staff.

The essence of such empowerment is a combination of self-sufficiency based on a solid foundation of training and management practices that ensure that staff will be able to do the right thing.

Letting go

Often, when I conduct training courses, the room is full of managers tied, as if by umbilical cord, to their mobile telephones or pagers. Many of the calls that are made in the breaks are not responses to messages, they are just to 'see everything is all right'. Are such calls, or the vast majority of them, really necessary? I wonder.

The opposite of this situation is more instructive. See if this rings a bell. You get back to the office after a gap (a business trip, holiday, whatever). Everything seems to be in order. When you examine some of the things that have been done you find that your view is that staff have made exactly the right decisions, yet . . . you know that *if you had been in the office, they would have asked you about some of the issues involved.* Some of the time staff empower themselves, and when they do, what they do is very often right.

All empowerment does is put this kind of process on a formal footing. It creates more self-reliant staff, able to consider what to do, make appropriate decisions and execute the necessary action successfully. Perhaps we should all allow this to happen more often and more easily.

Making empowerment possible

Empowerment cannot be seen as an isolated process. It is difficult to view it other than as an integral part of the overall management process.

You can only set out to create a feeling of empowerment by utilizing a range of other specific management processes to that end. Though the process perhaps starts with attitude and communication. What degree of autonomy do your staff feel you allow them? If they feel restricted and, worse, under your control every moment of the day, they will tend to perform less well. Allowing such feeling is certainly a good way to stifle initiative and creativity.

So you need to let it be known that you expect a high degree of self-sufficiency, and manage in a way that makes it possible. All sorts of things contribute, but the following are key:

- **Clear policy**: empowerment will only ever work if everyone understands the intentions of the organization (or department), their role (clear job descriptions) so as to allow them to take any action they may need to decide upon in context.

  The other requirement of an empowered group is an absence of detailed rules to be followed slavishly, but clear guidelines about the results to be aimed at.

- **good communication**: this has been mentioned before in the context of motivation. Any organization can easily be stifled by lack of, or lack of clarity in, communication; an empowered group is doubly affected by this failing.

- **little interference**: management must set things up so that people can be self-sufficient, and then keep largely clear. Developing the habit of taking the initiative is quickly stifled if staff know nothing they do will be able to be completed without endless checks (mostly, they will feel, made just at the wrong moment).

- **consultation**: a management style in which consultation is inherent acts as the best foundation for an empowered way of operating. It means that the framework within which people take responsibility is not simply wished, perhaps seemingly unthinkingly, upon them, but is something they helped define – and of which they have taken ownership.

- **feedback**: empowerment needs to maintain itself, actions taken must not sink into a rut and cease to be appropriate because time has passed and no one has considered the implications of change. Feedback may only be a manifestation of consultation, but some controls are also necessary. Certainly the overall ethos must be one of dynamism, continuing to search for better and better ways to do things as a response to external changes in a dynamic, and competitive, world.

- **development**: it is axiomatic that if people are to be empowered, they must be competent to execute the tasks required of them and do so well. This ties in with what has already been said about training and development earlier.

An enlightened attitude to development is motivational. A well-trained team of people are better able to be empowered, they have the confidence and the skills. An empowered and competent team is more likely to produce better productivity and performance. It is a virtuous circle.

At the end of the day the answer is in your hands. Keep too tight a reign on people and they will no doubt perform, but they may lack the enthusiasm to excel. Management should have nothing less than excellence of performance as its aim – market pressures mean any other view risks the organization being vulnerable to events and competitive action.

On the other hand, too little control, an abrogation of responsibility and control, also create risk. In this case that staff will fly off at a tangent, losing sight of their objectives and, worse, doing no more than what takes their fancy.

Like so much else in life, a balance is necessary. Empowerment is not a panacea, but an element of this philosophy can enhance the performance of most teams. Achievement and responsibility ranked high in the review of positive motivators in Chapter 3. Empowerment embodies both. Motivation will always remain a matter of detail, with management seeking to obtain the most powerful cumulative impact from the sum total of their actions, while keeping the time and cost of so doing within sensible bounds.

Empowerment is one more arrow in the armoury of potential techniques available to you, but it is an important one. Incorporate it in what becomes the right mix of ideas and methods for you, your organization and people and it can help make the whole thing work effectively.

AFTERWORD

It's a funny thing about life: if you
refuse to accept anything but the best,
you very often get it.

W. Somerset Maugham

All managers are ultimately judged on their results. Whether
you manage one other person, a small team or an entire
organization, you are dependent on the contribution others
make. And the quality of that contribution is dependent on
their motivation. People perform better when their motivation is high. What's more, the difference between adequate
performance and excellent performance spurred on by
motivation can be considerable.

Motivation works, but it is sometimes neglected. If so,
this is less likely to be because a manager has tried and
failed, more because they have found it difficult or incon-
venient and given up on it.

In fact, as this short book has been at pains to
demonstrate, motivation is not difficult. The principles are

common sense and there are plenty of ideas – many of them individually simple and straightforward – to help create a powerful, continuous positive motivational effect.

Like most managers, you are no doubt very busy. The greatest difficulty about motivation is perhaps simply the perceived difficulty of fitting it in. Yet the rewards make the time it takes well worthwhile, and the effect of the problems of a demotivated group of people on their manager's time are all too obvious.

Successful managers are good at motivation.

Ten ways to achieving adopting a motivational style may be summarized as follows:

1. Always think about the people aspects of everything.

2. Keep a list of possible motivational actions, large and small, in mind.

3. Monitor the 'motivational temperature' regularly.

4. See the process as continuous and cumulative.

5. Ring the changes in terms of method to maintain interest.

6. Do not be judgemental about what motivates others, either positively or negatively.

7. Beware of panaceas and easy options.

8. Make sufficient time for it.

9. Evaluate what works best within your group.

10. Remember that, in part at least, there should be a 'fun' aspect to work.

Make motivation a habit, take a creative approach to it and you may be surprised by what you can achieve. The motivation for you to motivate others is in the results.

So, if you have read this far – well done. If you now resolve to be more active in your motivational action – well done again. If you have a list of actions you want to take or areas you resolve to consider further (which is the best possible way to end any review) – another well done.

If, later, you find motivation of the people you work with improving, and results following the same path, that is down to you – and you can congratulate both your people and yourself.